T0276528

PLANTING
FOR
BUTTERFLIES

PLANTING
FOR
BUTTERFLIES

The Grower's Guide
to Creating a Flutter

JANE MOORE

ILLUSTRATED BY JAMES WESTON LEWIS

Hardie Grant

QUADRILLE

DEDICATION

For Paul, Anna, Theo and Keith.

CONTENTS

INTRODUCTION

When I started gardening professionally many years ago,
it wasn't simply a love of plants that spurred me into the job
– it was far more all-encompassing than that. I love the sense
of being part of nature that gardening brings, a connection
with the outdoors and all things within it.

Butterflies are an essential part of that cycle and you don't have
to spend long in a garden to meet one or two of them. There
are few things better in life than that simple harmony of the
natural world buzzing, fluttering and flitting about around you
as you weed, water and tend your little patch. I will never forget
my first encounter with an Orange Tip butterfly, both of us
soaking up the sunshine on that first, long-awaited warm day of
spring. That resulted in the purchase of my first butterfly book,
followed by swift identification of its caterpillar food plant, and
so a passion began.

In the UK we have 59 species of butterfly, most of them native to the country but with a couple of regular migrants. In the US the number of natives is a whopping 525 species or thereabouts, rising to 725 with seasonal migrants, although some are very localized inhabitants. Of course, worldwide there are far, far more, which makes butterfly spotting a rather marvellous passion that can travel with you far and wide.

Making a home for butterflies in your garden is easy to achieve and makes a lot of sense, as well as lending a new purpose to your choice of plants. Bring in the butterflies and you will be helping to build an entire ecosystem, from pollination for plants to prey for birds. Many of the plants loved by the common butterflies are remarkably simple to grow and common butterflies are obligingly easy to attract. Plant the right plants and the butterflies will come, believe me.

CHAPTER ONE

WHY SHOULD WE ENCOURAGE BUTTERFLIES?

P icture a long, lazy summer's day – clouds scudding across the blue sky, scents wafting on the breeze, birds singing and butterflies flitting from flower to flower. For many of us butterflies are simply an essential part of summer; a delicately beautiful part of nature that doesn't bite or sting, but simply adds more beauty to an already lovely season. It's impossible to imagine a world without them bringing colour, vibrancy and life to the garden. Yet we take them for granted, expecting them to flourish even though butterfly populations and their natural habitats are threatened more seriously year by year. In the UK alone, five species have become extinct in the past 150 years and several others have died out in particular regions. It might not seem to be a crisis, but more species are critically endangered now than ever before, with three-quarters of UK butterflies in decline.

The situation is just as worrying in the US, where at least five butterflies have become extinct since 1950, another 25 are presently listed as endangered nationwide, and four more are listed as threatened. NatureServe, one of the leading sources of information about rare and endangered species, assessed all of the roughly 700 or so butterfly species in the US and found that 17 per cent are at risk of extinction.

Modern farming practices, loss of habitat and global warming have all played a part. Habitats have been decimated on a huge scale, while climate change affects the lifecycle of the butterfly and its food plants enormously. Add to this pollution and shifting weather patterns and the butterfly's future has never been so precarious.

However, the situation is not all doom and gloom, as a broader awareness of the importance of these tiny building blocks of nature is growing all the time, at both national and international level. Most people really care about their local environment and we all have a greater sense of our individual, personal ability to improve things. We all feel that conservation begins at home and there is a sense that we're improving not only our own environment here and now, but also looking to the future.

Butterflies are our most beautiful insects. Referenced in literature, art and music, they are truly iconic and often portrayed as the very essence of nature. Even the smallest child knows a butterfly and its fascinating journey from egg to caterpillar, pupa to butterfly – a lifecycle often taught in schools to pique children's interest in the natural sciences.

The fascination with the butterfly's lifecycle extends well beyond childhood for some. Butterflies and moths are regarded by scientists and conservationists as highly sensitive indicators of the general health of the environment. Areas that are rich in butterflies are rich in other less obvious invertebrates (which make up over two thirds of all species), which makes for a healthy food chain and a vibrant ecosystem. Scientists use butterflies as model organisms to study the impact of climate changes, as well as habitat loss and their fragmentation, where habitats are partly destroyed, leaving behind smaller unconnected areas. It's their very fragility that makes them sensitive and quick to react to changes in their environment for good or bad. That makes their struggle to survive or ability to flourish a good measure of an area's environmental health and wellbeing. If there are fewer butterflies in your particular area than there used to be, then there is far more at stake than simply a loss of colour in the countryside.

Butterflies and moths are clear indicators of a healthy environment and healthy, sustainable ecosystems, providing plenty of other environmental benefits of which the most important is pollination of plants. Added to that, they are an essential element of the food chain and are prey for birds, bats and other insect-eating animals. As an example, in the UK and Ireland blue tits eat an estimated 50 billion moth caterpillars each year.

Conserving butterflies improves our whole environment, both personally and locally, not just for us individually but for those around us and hopefully for the generations to come. In fact, butterflies do add immeasurably to our positive feelings, improving our mental health as well as our physical health. Many of us love to get out into the fresh air at the weekend, gardening or walking in the countryside, often spotting butterflies, birds and other wildlife as we go along. Over 10,000 people take it one step further, recording butterflies and moths in the UK countryside on a regular basis on behalf of organizations such as Butterfly Conservation, with some 850 sites monitored each week.

While recording the butterfly activity on these precious ecosystems is proving invaluable right now, the study of butterflies is far from a recent occupation. Scientists, both professional and amateur, have been keeping records for hundreds of years and this provides a unique source of information and observation on this particular insect group which is unmatched in geographical scale and timescale anywhere in the world. This knowledge bank is proving extremely important for scientific research into climate change.

But conservation also offers something far more intangible than the obvious rewards. Butterflies symbolize something crucial about our quality of life: a sense of freedom, beauty and harmony with the natural world. It's no surprise that songs, plays, art and even advertisements use butterflies to make statements about peace, wellbeing and environmental values. There is something about the fragile beauty of the butterfly and its fleeting lifespan that reminds us of our own existence and how we need to take a moment to smell the flowers ourselves.

At home, our gardens are a tiny slice of that broader picture, a micro ecosystem within a larger ecosystem. My garden may be small but it's nonetheless an important and integral cog within that circle of life. Within its walls and hedges, butterflies live out their simple lives of feeding, mating and egg-laying on the flowers and plants that I have planted. It's not just my garden, it's theirs too.

CHAPTER TWO

TEN IMPORTANT FACTS TO KNOW ABOUT BUTTERFLIES

Known for their delicate, fluttering wings, butterflies conjure up images of meadows, summertime and warmth. Not only are they incredibly lovely to look at, they are long-distance travellers, masters of disguise and an essential indicator of a thriving environment. Here's a glimpse into some other remarkable facts about these truly complex creatures.

1 THEIR WINGS ARE ACTUALLY TRANSPARENT

Butterfly wings reflect light, meaning that they appear to be brilliantly coloured. If you look closely, you'll see that they actually have four wings rather than just two, and the wings are covered with tiny three-dimensional scales which reflect the light, causing the jewel-like iridescence. Over time these scales will rub off, which is why older butterflies often look more faded and dull. Beneath the scales is a transparent membrane which sometimes is revealed and is especially visible in the Glasswing butterfly (*Greta oto*), a native of South America. This iridescence is best shown off by the Purple Emperor butterfly (*Apatura iris*) where the deep purple-blue sheen on the wings of the male is only visible from certain angles and under bright lighting conditions.

THERE ARE A LOT OF THEM

Something like 18,500 named species of butterfly exist in the world and even more moths – about 140,000. Antarctica is the only continent where butterflies and moths have never been found. The largest butterfly is the Queen Alexandra's Birdwing (*Ornithoptera alexandrae*) with a wingspan of 25cm (10in), found in Papua New Guinea. In the US there are some 725 species with 525 regular inhabitants. In Europe there are almost 500 species, with 140 of those unique to Europe, while in the UK there are 59 resident species boosted by another half dozen or so that migrate from abroad and breed during the warmer months.

There are quite a few butterflies and moths that are spread widely throughout the world. For example, the Monarch (*Danaus plexippus*), the Plain Tiger (*Danaus chrysippus*) and the distinctly unglamorous Small White (*Pieris rapae*) are found on at least three continents. But it's the Painted Lady (*Vanessa cardui*) that holds the crown of being the more widely seen butterfly throughout the world. You will see Painted Lady anywhere from Alaska to the Caribbean and Venezuela, all though Europe and temperate Asia, from Africa to the Far East. Australia and New Zealand even have their own Painted Lady (*Vanessa kershawi*), which many regard as simply a sub species of *Vanessa cardui*.

3 THEY LOVE THE SUN

Butterflies are cold-blooded and love sunbathing so you'll
often see them basking on a sunny day, wings open to catch
the warmth. They actually need to maintain a surprisingly high
body temperature to keep on flying, around 30°C (87°F), and
they do this by absorbing the sunshine, although some species
seem to bask more than others. Red Admirals (*Vanessa atalanta*)
are especially keen on this and their dark wings are ideal for
soaking up the rays. On the flip side, butterflies really don't
like cold, windy, drizzly days and there are only a few species
you will see flying in that kind of weather. If it's too chilly,
they become completely immobile.

4 THEY ARE MASTERS OF DISGUISE

Butterflies hide themselves in all sorts of clever ways, pretending
to be a spring leaf in the case of the Brimstone (*Gonepteryx
rhamni*) which even has raised 'veins' on its wings to complete
the disguise. Comma (*Polygonia c-album*) butterflies have
beautifully coloured upper wings, but once they're closed
they look just like raggedy old
dried leaves. Other butterflies
adopt camouflage techniques,
such as Small Whites who hide
themselves cleverly in white
flowers, while the mottled
underwings of the Orange Tip
(*Anthocharis cardamines*) hide it
beautifully amongst the white
flowers of garlic mustard, one of
its main food plants.

5 THEY DON'T EAT

Butterflies can only actually drink, sucking nectar, rotting fruit and water through their straw-like proboscis. This is one of the first parts of the butterfly to develop during metamorphosis – when they first emerge it's in two parts which have to be joined together, so you'll often see a newly emerged butterfly coiling and uncoiling its proboscis to test it. The proboscis is longer in some species than others, so some butterflies aren't able to reach the nectar in flowers which have deep tubes. When it's not needed, the proboscis curls up neatly.

Nectar provides everything the butterfly needs to live its short but dynamic life. As well as sugar and water, it contains lots of nutrients such as amino acids, proteins, enzymes and vitamins. Once a flower's nectar supply has been exhausted, the butterfly will move on, which is why it's essential to provide a rich and steady supply of flowering plants.

6 THEY NEED WATER

You'll often spot butterflies drinking from puddles or wet soil and these are usually the male of the species. That's because there are minerals and salts dissolved in the water which are thought to be essential to their fertility.

7 THEY ARE GOOD AT SCARING PREDATORS

Many butterflies have distinctive eyespots or 'ocelli' on their wings which are especially designed to ward off inquisitive birds and predators. While most patterns develop to hide the butterfly from predators, these eyespots actually draw attention to the insect, which means they must be particularly effective as evolution would have put paid to them if they didn't work.

Not all butterflies and moths use their eyespots in the same way, though. Some have them on show all the time, such as the Peacock butterfly (*Inachis io*), while others like the Bullseye moth (*Automeris io*) keep their eyespots hidden beneath forewings which have the appearance of a dead leaf, only flashing them when disturbed, to surprise and scare the predator. Many of the eyespots are rather beautiful, featuring concentric circles of rich colours, often with a white dot or flash in the centre which mimics an eye reflecting light. Evolution is really very clever.

8 THEY TASTE WITH THEIR FEET

Butterflies have senses of taste, smell and touch, but their 'taste buds' are in their feet. This is very handy for finding out if the leaf they're on is good enough to lay their eggs on. Once the eggs hatch that leaf is their offspring's first meal, so it's vitally important to make sure it's a good one, and the taste receptors on the butterfly's feet will tell it the leaf is healthy and free of toxins.

⑨ THEY CAN MIGRATE HUGE DISTANCES

Some adult butterflies migrate to avoid the cold weather, sometimes incredibly long distances. The Monarch butterfly (*Danaus plexippus*) travels something like 3,000 miles (4,800km) from Canada to Mexico in a mass migration in the autumn. In 1924, one flight of Painted Lady in California was estimated to contain about 3,000 million butterflies. But some butterflies travel no distance at all, living out their entire lives from egg though to adult in the same little habitat.

⑩ THEY HAVE POOR EYESIGHT

Butterflies are near sighted and so a nice big bed of colourful flowers will attract them into your garden. Plant flowers in blocks and plant for a succession of flowering to keep them happy. Choose their favourite shades of pink, purple, yellow and white (avoid red as they are basically blind to this colour) – and go for single blooms rather than double as not only is the nectar hard to reach in a double flower, but they also have less. Flower size isn't important; many herbs have very small flowers but are rich in good-quality nectar.

Butterflies actually have a keener sense of smell than sight and use this to help locate nectar plants. A good strong scent increases the likelihood of a butterfly visiting a flower, thus improving the chance of the flower being successfully pollinated. Once that's happened a flower loses its scent as its job is done and now the plant concentrates on developing the seed and fruit, which is why regular deadheading is essential for both gardeners and butterflies.

Anatomy of a butterfly

a. antenna club ; b. compound eye ; c. head ; d. proboscis ;
e. thorax ; f. tibia ; g. tarsus ; h. femur ; i. abdomen ; j. hindwing ;
k. forewing ; l. outer margin ; m. coastal margin

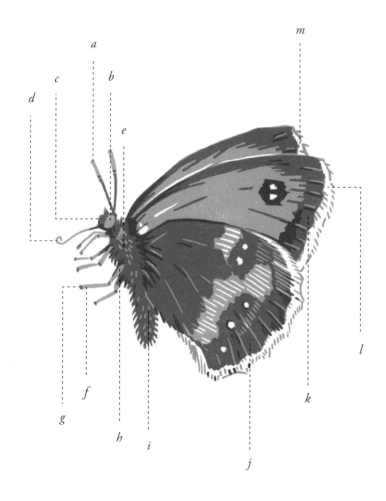

a

c

b

d

e

m

f

g

h

i

j

k

l

CHAPTER THREE

THE LIFE OF A BUTTERFLY

One of the things that draws us towards butterflies is that their existence is so fleeting – their lives are here today and gone tomorrow. Yet for such a short lifespan they adorn the landscape magnificently, adding an immeasurable brightness and vivacity to the garden.

THE MATING GAME

Essentially butterflies exist only to find a mate and reproduce, often a somewhat frenetic and fleeting existence. Most live for only a few weeks, although some can overwinter and sometimes you'll find a Peacock or a Painted Lady tucked away in a dry corner of your shed, trying to while the winter away. Some are so short-lived it really is only a matter of days – my beloved Orange Tip has a blink-and-you'll-miss-it 18 days to pack in a whirlwind romance. Nature provides a marvellous dating service though and, all being well, they'll find their mates. It starts with a predilection towards the same host plants, fluttering around to identify each other by visual clues, such as distinct wing markings. Pheromones (complex chemical indicators similar to a scent) also come into play to signal that they're ready to mate.

It's this hosting which is important for gardeners as particular butterflies, and their offspring, will be drawn towards individual plants. Understandably the adults need to feed regularly with their short but energetic lives, so planting a selection – and a succession – of host plants increases your chances of attracting a good variety of butterflies to wine, dine and romance their partners in your garden.

Butterflies mate either on the ground or in the air while fluttering and the internal fertilization of the eggs takes anything from a few seconds to many minutes or hours. Six Spot Burnet moths are blissfully distracted for hours when mating, so much so that they're a piece of cake to photograph as they share a cosy stem together, oblivious to everything but each other.

After the fun is over, the female butterfly searches for the right type of plant to lay her eggs on, sensing it with her feet and laying eggs singly or in clusters. This host plant will provide food for the emerging caterpillars once they hatch and so the cycle begins once again.

FROM EGG
TO BUTTERFLY

EGG

Female butterflies lay many eggs in their short lives to ensure that even a few of them will survive. From adverse weather conditions to parasitizing insects, among other things, the chances of hatching successfully as a caterpillar, let alone getting through pupation to the adult butterfly stage, are pretty fraught with danger – although sometimes that's hard to believe after seeing a crop of cabbage plants ravaged by a horde of Large White caterpillars almost overnight.

Some butterflies lay single eggs on the host plants, flitting from one leaf to another, while others lay small clusters of eggs and some lay hundreds at a time. Even the eggs have significant characteristics so you can recognize many species in this way, if you're so inclined. For example, Large White butterfly eggs are tall, yellow and ridged, laid in orderly groups of 60 or so on the top of a brassica leaf, while the Orange Tip lays single eggs near the flowers and buds of its host plant. Lots of butterfly caterpillars are nettle eaters and so it's no surprise that many lay their eggs in patches of stinging nettles. The Peacock lays batches of small eggs in clusters under the nettle leaf, while the Red Admiral lays a single egg at a time on the upper surface of the leaf.

CATERPILLAR

Once hatched, most caterpillars vary distinctly from one another so they're often easy to identify. Many are vividly coloured and scarily hairy, such as the Painted Lady and the Peacock, although the strangest-looking caterpillars are nearly always moth larvae. Others, such as the Red Admiral, wrap themselves protectively in a little individual tent of nettle leaves while feeding on the nettle. Some camouflage themselves beautifully to look just like a leaf, such as the Brimstone and the Small White, and these two do look very alike, so you need to pay attention to the host plant. A Small White caterpillar will be on a cabbage or something from the same plant family.

Many butterflies and moths spend a great part of their active lives as a caterpillar, often feeding and growing, shedding their skins as they get fatter. The Fox moth lives as a caterpillar for about 11 months before becoming an adult, but for some it's a pretty quick turnaround, such the Painted Lady butterfly which spends a scant four weeks as a caterpillar.

There are also many more caterpillars that will never become adult butterflies. Most will be picked off by birds or other predators or die from natural infections by viruses, bacteria and fungi. Such is the cycle of life. But in the meantime, spring and summer find plants in gardens, parks and hedgerows alive with the steady munching of millions of caterpillars.

PUPA

Surely one of the strangest stages of any lifecycle in the animal kingdom, the pupa is the stage where the caterpillar transforms or pupates into a chrysalis or cocoon from which an adult butterfly or moth of a completely different shape emerges. Chrysalises are the pupal casings of butterflies, while moth pupae are encased in cocoons. You'll find pupae hanging from plants or fence posts, in sheds or stuck to a stem of grass, and they often look very alike, which makes it hard to identify the occupant. A few are distinctive, such as the yellow papery cocoon of the Burnet moth attached to a knapweed, plantain or grass stem, but most resemble a leaf or a twig and you simply won't notice them.

EMERGENCE

Once inside the chrysalis, it all becomes a kind of 'soup' for a while as the 'organizer' cells form the vital parts of the adult body. You can often see the colours of the wings just before hatching, but once they're out of that protective shell it's a very dangerous time for the butterfly. Drying the wings can take a couple of hours, during which time they're vulnerable to predators. As soon as it can fly, the butterfly is off to find some nectar and a mate, hopefully in your garden.

CHAPTER FOUR

CATERPILLARS AND THEIR NEEDS

The four stages of life for a butterfly (see pages 30–32) are fraught with danger but, while there is little you can do for a chrysalis, you can provide a good spot for the adults to lay their eggs and a good feeding station for the ensuing caterpillars. It's a question of keeping the caterpillar happy and hopefully that will lead to fully-fledged adult butterflies making merry in your garden, producing eggs and so on.

Butterflies are naturally drawn to the food plants for their offspring, laying eggs directly on the leaf so the almost blind, stumpy-legged caterpillars merely need to emerge from their eggs to start feeding. In fact, most start by eating their own egg casings as they hatch. Many caterpillars, such as the Blues, live solitary lives, going through the several stages of growth and moulting, or shedding their skins as they grow, completely alone. Having said that, there are some Blues that spend part of their caterpillar life being looked after by ants in exchange for feeding them from a 'honey gland' on their bodies. The ants get well fed and so does the caterpillar, as well as nicely protected from predators and parasites – one of the strange but wonderful partnerships the natural world excels in.

However, there are lots of species that live in large groups, including Peacocks and, of course, the infamous Large Whites laying waste to your cabbages. A few caterpillars live in great silken nests which you sometimes see suspended in trees and hedgerows. Mostly these are moth caterpillars, but a few butterflies such as the Black-Veined White also do this for protection.

Caterpillars don't move far – they're not designed for travel – so most of the time when you see a caterpillar making a bold journey across your garden path or lawn it's on its way to pupate, which they tend to do some distance away from the feeding ground. Many caterpillars will crawl a significant way in search of that perfect spot for pupation. Of course, once they're in the chrysalis they have no defence whatsoever against the vagaries of weather, diseases or predators. It's an instinct for self-preservation that sends caterpillars on these epic marches to find a suitably sheltered spot which could be underground, in a folded leaf or attached to leaves, stems, twigs, fences or garden buildings. Despite the caterpillars' best efforts, many are still picked off by predators. In fact, blue tits are known to make an easy summer meal from the chrysalises of Small Tortoiseshell butterflies hanging under the eaves of garden sheds or window sills. But once the caterpillars have pupated, the chrysalises are there to stay for anything from a few days to several months depending on the species, before finally emerging as a butterfly if all goes well.

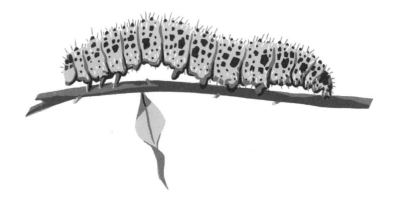

FOOD PLANTS

Caterpillars are very limited in their diet and many species will only eat the leaves of a single type of plant. There is little doubt that the plant that a butterfly first ate as a caterpillar strongly influences the plant that it later lays its eggs on.

This is good news for gardeners as it means we can target butterflies by growing 'their' food plants. Sadly it's also bad news as many of these plants are not ones we would want to grow at all. For example, take buckthorn, an unprepossessing shrub unless you're a female Brimstone butterfly, in which case it is the only viable home and hearth for the eggs and progeny of your brief liaison. Stinging nettles, which gardeners abhor and rush to remove should they spot any, are a favourite nursery ground for many of our most majestic butterflies, including the Peacock and Red Admiral. No matter how keen a butterfly gardener you are, I don't think you'll want to cultivate nettles in your garden and I can't blame you.

However, there are many butterflies that will lay their eggs on a wide range of food plants, for example the Holly Blue will lay its eggs on holly, ivy and some dogwood species, while the Painted Lady is extremely easy-going and favours a wide range of plants including aster, borage, marigold and many, many more. Most butterflies have a few food plants their caterpillars will eat and some of these you can happily incorporate into the garden – even some of the wilder species work well, especially in a dedicated wild area. And don't forget that butterflies themselves are extremely mobile creatures, migrating long distances to find a mate, so plant a nectar-rich garden for the adult butterflies and they will come.

CREATING A GOOD HABITAT

The good thing about butterflies is that, unlike most caterpillars, they're not fussy about their food. As long as there are plenty of nectar-rich flowers blooming at the right time they will flutter about your garden in carefree abandon. So it's pretty straightforward to create a lovely space to attract them to feed. Providing an accommodating environment for them to lay their eggs and for their caterpillars to feed and pupate is something else again. The ideal 'garden' would be something of a wild one: dense swathes of stinging nettles, a sweep of wildflower-dotted meadow and some sprawling patches of brambles – not really the look that I'm going for in my garden and I expect you feel the same!

But there are some simple things we can do to attract the butterflies to spend their whole life cycles in our garden. Plant a holly or one of the many ornamental varieties of ivy – both are host plants for the Holly Blue young. Add a few violets into a shady border to encourage Fritillary butterflies. Plant some sweet rocket or honesty, both worthwhile garden plants in their own right and brilliantly attractive to adult butterflies, but also food plants for the Green Veined White butterfly and, more wonderfully, the Orange Tip.

In the kitchen garden try growing nasturtiums as a sacrificial crop for the White butterfly caterpillars – they look great and their presence does at least spread the caterpillars' attentions – while borage is good for Fritillaries and sorrel for Small Coppers.

But probably the single best thing you can do is to let your lawn grow a bit long. I know it goes against the grain but just do it in certain places – perhaps let the grasses flower in odd corners. There are so very many butterflies that count grass as their food plants, including the Gatekeeper, the Meadow Brown, the Speckled Wood, the Heaths and the Skippers. Push your own boundaries by planting a few wild flowers around the edges and hedges, or go for it and develop a little meadow of your very own. Allow the clover to come back into your grass for the Clouded Yellows, add in some bird's-foot trefoil for the Common Blue and nurture the knapweed for the glorious day-flying Burnet moths.

BREEDING BUTTERFLIES

There's no doubt that the best way to appreciate butterflies is in their natural environment. It's such a wonderful thing to see which butterflies choose your garden after all your efforts to make it a perfect place for them. The simple pleasure of seeing a butterfly feeding at a flower, or watching it courting, is a million times more satisfying than looking at a butterfly in a cage, or a dead specimen in a display case.

If you're impatient, you can also buy caterpillars online to rear yourself – a fascinating thing to do, especially with children. There is also a trend for buying butterflies for releasing at a wedding but this seems somewhat flippant considering they're living creatures, especially if they are the more tropical species which will be killed off by the first blast of cool weather. But having said that, the only way to re-colonize areas where butterfly species have died out is through carefully managed breeding programmes. For most of us, these online caterpillars provide a great opportunity to watch caterpillars of more commonplace species go through the whole fascinating metamorphosis process, naturally releasing the butterflies into the garden at the end.

BREEDING YOUR OWN

There are lots of internet sites selling larvae or you can seek out some eggs in the wild, especially as some of the easiest to rear are the nettle-dwellers such as Red Admiral, Small Tortoiseshell and Painted Lady.

- You'll need a cage measuring about 60 x 60cm (24 x 24in), 90cm (36in) tall – a sturdy frame securely covered with net curtaining on a solid base is ideal. You can buy them with a zip fastening for easy access or make your own.

- You'll also need some food plants such as nettles growing in large pots, at least three plants covering around three-quarters of the cage space should be enough for the caterpillars to feed on before they pupate (but have a few spares to hand as well).

- Make sure you don't touch the larvae or eggs when you place them on the food plants – use a leaf or a paintbrush – as they will think you are a predator and react accordingly.

- Place the plants on newspaper so you can change it regularly – caterpillars are eating machines and what goes in inevitably comes out. If they eat their way through a plant, just add another plant into the cage and they will find it.

- The larvae will grow for about three weeks, shedding their skins several times, before they pupate in the cage. They'll stay as a chrysalis for 10–14 days before emerging as an adult butterfly. You can set them free immediately or wait until they've mated and laid eggs once again on the food plants so you can start the whole process again.

This is a great project to do with children, but don't consider it as a sustainable way to introduce butterflies into your garden. Many of the captive-bred butterflies are weaker than wild species and may not thrive. It's infinitely better to set about creating a varied, nectar-rich habitat in your garden which will attract the wild butterflies to mate naturally.

CHAPTER FIVE

WHAT CAN I DO IN MY GARDEN?

A garden might initially seem far too small a space to provide much of a sanctuary for butterflies, but even a small outdoor area holds a huge amount of potential, especially when you think of gardens linking together across a built-up environment. Urban oases and green corridors have become increasingly important for wildlife in general, and butterflies are no exception. Where there is a need to build more housing in towns and cities, gardens provide essential pit stops for wildlife, linking together parks, canals, rivers and any green spaces.

In the countryside too, monoculture farming of single species such as wheat, alongside an over-reliance on pesticides, has made farmland akin to deserts for wildlife. Couple this with the destruction of hedges that has taken place over the past 50 years to make way for huge fields that can be serviced by large-scale machinery and it's no wonder that our gardens are becoming a repository of plant and insect variety. Butterflies and creatures of all sorts will visit any garden, urban or countryside, tiny or vast, as long as it offers them what they need. For butterflies that's very simple – they need plenty of nectar-rich flowers and food plants for their caterpillars.

GREEN CORRIDORS

In fact, it's in our towns and cities that much-needed action is happening. In some, urban planners are purposely creating 'green' or 'wildlife' corridors but in many places it happens via a more haphazard linking of gardens without specific planning. Green corridors are strips of land deliberately left undeveloped to bridge wildlife habitats that have been divided by human development, such as roads or building projects. It's increasingly recognized that if this green corridor isn't left, then the wildlife populations can become unstable and that some species of animals, insects and plants could become threatened. These green corridors allow the animals to migrate to new areas, often improving the plant populations indirectly by allowing greater pollination and taking seeds into new areas.

THE GARDEN ECOSYSTEM

We tend to think of an ecosystem as a large area – imagine a woodland or a range of mountains – but, although they can be as big as that, an ecosystem can also be as tiny as a pond in your garden. All an ecosystem really consists of is a group of plants and animals that share the same resources and depend on one another for survival. The ecosystem we're trying to evolve to keep our butterflies happy is a simple equation of providing plenty of flowers for nectar, good food plants for egg laying and the subsequent caterpillars, and safe havens for chrysalises. You can create a good ecosystem in a small garden and a brilliant one for all sorts of butterflies in a large garden, but even a window box full of the right flowers can provide an essential pit stop for butterflies flitting from one habitat to another.

CREATING HABITATS

Think of your garden as a series of mini ecosystems which all link up to provide a whole panoply of offerings to tempt butterflies and other wildlife. While plenty of flowers are the key factor for many of the most spectacular garden butterflies, other butterflies are very specific in their preferred habitats.

With a meadow you can also lure in many of the grassland types, such as the Common Blue and the Meadow Brown. It doesn't need to be big, but it does need to have a variety of plants and flowering grasses. Creating a meadow isn't simply a case of letting the grass grow. Buy and plant plugs of wildflowers, then allow them to seed before you cut the meadow at the end of the summer and try to leave one or two patches of long grass through the winter.

Hedges, especially flowering ones, provide food and shelter for caterpillars and adult butterflies, but add wildflowers to the base and you're creating a great habitat for more shade-loving butterflies, such as the Speckled Wood and the Ringlet.

Flower borders need to be filled from spring to autumn with a range of flowering, nectar-rich plants which are simply irresistible to butterflies. The kitchen garden can be overflowing with a riot of herbs and annual flowers and some fruit left unpicked to feed the late butterflies. It's simply a case of trying to manage your garden from a butterfly's point of view.

BE GREEN

Gardening is all about control. If you think about it, a garden is nothing more than an engineered ecosystem with us gardeners playing the role of the engine drivers. A good gardener lets nature work for them, making the most of natural processes and using the least invasive and most sustainable techniques. Simply put, that means cutting down on the use of pesticides and herbicides as much as possible. Alongside killing pests and weeds, these also kill butterflies, moths and many other pollinating insects, as well as natural predators of pests, such as ground beetles, ladybirds and lacewings.

We're encouraged to create a nice, tidy garden, free of weeds, with well-managed lawns and borders, but is that really the best habitat for butterflies? It's a matter of changing your mindset, thinking less about order and more about nature, with a view to cultivating a wildlife-friendly environment. Butterflies aren't bothered whether their nectar comes from a fantastic flower border or a few weeds, just as long as it's there.

Every little bit we do to reduce our impact on the environment really does make a difference. For example, peat bogs are such important environments for many plants and animals, including several butterflies which are in decline such as the Large Heath. There are lots of great sustainable potting composts available nowadays which makes it easy to stop using peat-based compost.

Better still, start making your own compost and use this to feed your soil rather than commercial fertilizers. It's very easy to do and your own compost will be rich in organic matter, invertebrates and valuable natural minerals. It is far better for improving the overall soil structure than anything you can buy. Add to that the fact that it saves you money and it is the perfect way to recycle garden waste. It's also surprisingly satisfying and, although you might not be able to create a meadow or plant an orchard, making your own compost is nature at its most productive and attainable.

CHAPTER SIX

THE GARDENER'S FAVOURITE BUTTERFLIES, MOTHS AND PLANTS

B utterflies live life in the fast lane, feeding, fluttering and flirting for all they're worth during their brief lives. They seem to flit from flower to flower in a fairly indiscriminate way and it's true that all they really want from a flower is plenty of non-stop nectar, but nonetheless there are certain flowers and certain colours that pique their interest.

Due to their specialized mouthparts – a straw-like proboscis which uncurls to feed – butterflies can only sip nectar, the liquid from rotting fruit and mineral-rich water from pollen. In fact, some moths never feed at all, instead surviving on energy stored pre-pupation to see them through finding a mate and reproducing, after which they die. However, there are certain plants that suit this strange appendage better than others. For example, buddleia has lots of very nectar-rich flowers clustered together on each flower spike and each flower is a tubular shape – a perfect fit for the butterfly proboscis. No wonder it's a hit with them, although it's not popular with every butterfly species as some have shorter tongues than others (such as the Gatekeeper and Speckled Wood) and these are rarely seen on a buddleia.

Flower colour plays its part, too. Butterflies prefer blue, pink and purple blooms rather than bright reds and oranges. White is sometimes chosen by them, sometimes not, but what really matters to butterflies is quite simple and potentially achievable for gardeners with even quite a modest-sized urban space. And that is nothing more than growing a good variety of nectar-rich plants in a warm, sunny spot so the butterflies don't have to travel next door to find their lunch.

THE GARDENER'S FAVOURITE BUTTERFLIES

Every garden is different in terms of its soil, shelter, aspect and, of course, location. However, there are some things that remain fundamentally the same and some butterflies that are more likely to frequent your garden than others. Some of them are just plain common but nonetheless attractive such as the Meadow Brown, while others, such as the Peacock, are so bold and beautiful that they're probably the reason you bought this book in the first place. Some, like the Red Admiral, are hugely wide ranging, living in habitats from seashore to mountainside, in urban gardens and the countryside too.

This section is designed to help you single out those butterflies that have arrived in your garden so that you can identify them with conviction. All of them are butterflies that feed from garden plants and grasses that are easy to grow, and all add colour and vibrancy to the garden, even the Whites.

SMALL TORTOISESHELL
(AGLAIS URTICAE)

One of the most common and easiest butterflies
to recognize, the Small Tortoiseshell has an unusual
courtship technique. The butterflies tend to hang about
around nettle patches which are the food plants for Small
Tortoiseshell caterpillars. The male occupies a territory
close to a good nettle patch and, once he's attracted a mate,
he gets her in the mood by drumming his antennae on her hind
wings, making a faint noise which it's possible to hear should
you creep up on the romantic couple. The coquettish female
will then flutter off a little distance, pursued by her Romeo, and
the drumming begins again. The whole wooing process can go on
for several hours.

TIMING: The adults emerge from hibernation in spring and, as
there are two or three generations each summer, they're a common
sight. They hibernate as butterflies and can start hibernating as early
as late summer, often entering houses and resting in corners or under
pelmets as well as garages and garden sheds.

CATERPILLAR FOOD PLANTS: The caterpillars favour
hops and nettles and live in large silk nests on the food plant until
sufficiently grown to disperse and pupate.

BUTTERFLY FOOD PLANTS: The adults are common on
many garden plants, especially in late summer and autumn, including
ice plant, buddleia and echinacea.

RANGE: All of the UK, Europe and temperate regions of Asia, as
well as North America.

RED ADMIRAL
(VANESSA ATALANTA)

Such a beauty and so easy to identify
with its dark, almost black, wings boldly
striped with red which earned it the original
name of 'Admirable' in the 18th century. The
Red Admiral is a regular visitor to our gardens,
alighting on many plants and flowers as well as
having something of a penchant for rotting fruit
in autumn – a good reason not to tidy up those
fallen apples too briskly. We usually see it most
plentifully in the late summer and early
autumn on all sorts of garden plants, as well
as out in the countryside. It's a fast flyer and
patrols small territories such as sections of
garden or hedgerow, chasing away other butterflies.
It also loves to rest and bask in the sun, showing off its lovely
wings. Very rarely you may find one overwintering in the shed,
but usually the cold weather finishes them off.

TIMING: The first migrants arrive in the UK from central Europe
in late spring, laying eggs for a summer generation who are often seen
flying into late autumn.

CATERPILLAR FOOD PLANTS: The caterpillars live on
stinging nettles and occasionally hops.

BUTTERFLY FOOD PLANTS: The adults feed on a very wide
range of garden plants including buddleia, aster and ice plant.

RANGE: The UK, Europe, the Canary Islands, North Africa
and into Asia.

BRIMSTONE
(GONEPTERYX RHAMNI)

One of the first butterflies to emerge in spring and startlingly lovely with its beautiful colour and sharply pointed wings. The word 'butterfly' was probably first used to describe this buttery yellow beauty. With it's wings spread, this large lemon yellow male is unmistakable, while the female is a plain cream with no black markings. The first butterflies often emerge as leaves are unfurling in the spring and their large size and brilliant colour make them heralds of spring, although they fly all summer long and hibernate through the winter.

TIMING: They emerge from hibernation in spring and the males are most commonly seen then, as they're seeking a mate. The new generation appears in summer and feeds until their autumn hibernation, when the adult butterfly emerges, beautifully camouflaged and hidden among holly or ivy leaves.

CATERPILLAR FOOD PLANTS:
The caterpillars feed on only two shrubs, buckthorn and alder buckthorn, neither of which are good garden plants.

BUTTERFLY FOOD PLANTS:
While the caterpillars are picky, the adults are far more adventurous in their food plants and are especially keen on purple flowers such as thistles and knapweeds, as well as being one of the main pollinators of primroses in spring.

RANGE: All of the UK, Europe and North Africa, as well as parts of Asia and as far as Japan.

GATEKEEPER
(PYRONIA TITHONUS)

One of the LBJs, as I tend to think of them (the 'little brown jobs'), which are hard to identify as there are several which are frustratingly rather similar. The Gatekeeper is fond of gateways and field edges and tends to feed and bask with open wings, unlike the Meadow Brown and the Ringlet (see pages 72 and 74) which often have their wings closed. To add to the confusion, the colouring and patterning of the wings are very variable too, but the open wings are a giveaway, as are the double white pupils in the eyes.

TIMING: One of the most common butterflies in the UK, you'll see Gatekeepers flying from early until late summer, even though each adult only lives for about three weeks. The caterpillars hibernate through the winter, low down among the grass.

CATERPILLAR FOOD PLANTS: Gatekeeper caterpillars live on grasses.

BUTTERFLY FOOD PLANTS: The adults are common in meadows or wild areas, as well as on brambles. Although it is a butterfly of grassy areas, nonetheless it's a common visitor to gardens and is especially fond of nectar-rich herbs such as marjoram and mint.

RANGE: Southern half of the UK and central and southern Europe.

PAINTED LADY
(VANESSA CARDUI)

A regular visitor to our gardens, this elegant butterfly is a common sight throughout the temperate world, although often looking a little tattered and torn. You won't find it in cold climates or in South America, nor will it overwinter in chillier climates such as the UK and most of Europe. The Painted Lady is very strong flyer and migrates in huge numbers to the UK in late spring from Southern Europe and North Africa where she breeds year round – a distance of more than 600 miles (965km). Every few years the migration populations are huge, with some reaching the Shetland Islands and even Iceland.

TIMING: Early migrant adults lay eggs on a wide variety of host plants, giving rise to a second generation of adults in late summer and autumn which will die out once the cold weather arrives.

CATERPILLAR FOOD PLANTS: The caterpillars aren't fussy eaters and will happily live on stinging nettles, thistles, mallows, agricultural crops and wildflowers.

BUTTERFLY FOOD PLANTS: The adults are extremely easy to please and very ready to feed after all that flying. They will happily settle wherever there is a good range of nectar plants such as buddleia, tree mallow, aster, goldenrod and many other garden plants.

RANGE: The whole of the UK and Europe, as well as North America and North Africa.

ORANGE TIP
(ANTHOCHARIS CARDAMINES)

A harbinger of spring, the Orange Tip is a distinctive sight with its orange-tipped white wings. Only the male has these orange tips on their wings, though, and the plain white female with her black tips can look a little like the Large White so don't mistake them. Both male and females have a mottled green camouflage to the underside of the wings which makes them easy to identify.

TIMING: Each adult only flies for about three weeks from spring to mid summer. After that, the caterpillars spend the summer feasting and then undergo a long pupation though autumn and winter until the warmer weather begins the cycle once again.

CATERPILLAR FOOD PLANTS: The caterpillars live on a number of very common wild plants such as hedge mustard, cuckoo flower and watercress.

BUTTERFLY FOOD PLANTS:
The adults are happy on garden plants such as sweet rocket, honesty and lilac.

RANGE: The UK, Europe and parts of Asia.

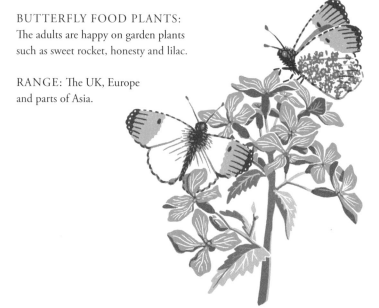

PEACOCK
(INACHIS IO)

The dramatic Peacock with its bright, eyed wings is one of the first butterflies you'll learn to recognize. Not only is it a common garden visitor with a habit of overwintering, but it has a long life assisted by its ability to scare off potential predators, such as birds, by flicking its wings open suddenly and flashing the eyespots. It also deters mammals such as mice and bats from taking too much interest in the winter months by making a hissing sound.

TIMING: Peacocks can live for almost a year as an adult butterfly, flying from mid summer to autumn. They hibernate in the corners of sheds and outhouses, even coming into houses and conservatories, and emerge in spring for a last blast of courtship.

CATERPILLAR FOOD PLANTS: Peacock caterpillars live on nettles, especially stinging nettles.

BUTTERFLY FOOD PLANTS: The adults are commonly found on many garden flowers, especially buddleia and ice plant, and on rotten fruit.

RANGE: A large butterfly and a strong flyer, the Peacock can cover long distances and is common in all of the UK and Europe, apart from the very coldest areas.

CABBAGE WHITE
(PIERIS BRASSICAE/PIERIS RAPAE)

For many gardeners this is the first butterfly they learn to spot, fluttering among their young cabbage plants as they lay their eggs. But there are actually two types of butterfly commonly called the Cabbage White – the Large White and the Small White. The caterpillars of both are equally rapacious, the Large White swiftly reducing plants to a skeleton of veins while the Small White caterpillars feed safely out of sight in the heart of the cabbage. To add to this, they lay eggs in their hundreds and usually produce a later generation in high summer, with the black markings on the wings of the Large White becoming more marked in this later batch.

TIMING: Large and Small Whites first appear from mid spring, with the second generation around until mid autumn. Populations of Large White are often boosted in summer by migration from the south. In spring it's possible to confuse the Whites with the female Brimstone (see page 65) but this has sharply pointed wing tips rather than rounded wings and a creamy colouring.

CATERPILLAR FOOD PLANTS: Actually neither caterpillars nor adults are fussy about food plants – any brassica will do, as well as crambe and nasturtiums in the garden.

BUTTERFLY FOOD PLANTS: As easy to please as their offspring, the adult Whites will feed on anything from lavender to bedding plants.

RANGE: The UK, Europe and parts of Asia and North Africa.

HOLLY BLUE
(CELASTRINA ARGIOLUS)

It's arguable which blue butterfly you're most likely to spot in your garden, but the likelihood is that it's the Holly Blue. Both the male and female of this butterfly are the most beautiful summer sky blue, with the female having distinctive blackened wing tips. It's a high flyer, fluttering up around the tops of trees and shrubs, and congregates around holly in the spring and ivy later on in the season, while the other grassland blues (such as Common Blue, Adonis Blue and Chalkhill Blue) tend to be low flyers.

TIMING: Two different generations means that you're likely to see the Holly Blue flying from spring through to autumn. It's particularly easy to identify in the spring as it emerges before any of the other blue butterflies.

CATERPILLAR FOOD PLANTS: Unusually the caterpillars have two different yet very specific host plants for the two different generations each year. The first spring hatchings live on holly, the buds swelling in time for this spring generation, while ivy buds are on the menu for the summer one. If neither plant is available, the caterpillars will feed on many other garden plants including dogwood, spindle and snowberry but it's not often necessary as holly and ivy abound.

BUTTERFLY FOOD PLANTS: Many garden plants will attract the adult butterfly but you'll often find them fluttering about hedges and shrubberies due to its preference for laying eggs on holly and ivy.

RANGE: The UK, Europe except the colder regions, and parts of Asia and North Africa.

MEADOW BROWN
(MANIOLA JURTINA)

One of the most common butterflies in central Europe, this is by far the most common butterfly in the UK. It's another LBJ or 'little brown job' but is easily recognized by its folded wings and eyespots with single white pupils. It's also darker and, well, browner than the Gatekeeper's lively orange (see page 66). The male is a dark dusky brown with single eyespots but, unusually for butterflies, the female is brighter than the male with a broad splash of orange on each forewing. Not only is the Meadow Brown the most commonly spotted butterfly in any location or habitat but it also makes a habit of flying on dull days – even in drizzle – when most other butterflies are nowhere to be seen.

TIMING: The adults emerge from early summer until mid autumn.

CATERPILLAR FOOD PLANTS: The caterpillars feed on many species of grass over an eight- or nine-month period, including throughout the winter.

BUTTERFLY FOOD PLANTS:
Adult butterflies feed from many garden plants including grasses, lavender, buddleia and herbs, as well as thistles and brambles.

RANGE: The UK, Europe and parts of Asia and North Africa.

OTHER BUTTERFLIES YOU'RE LIKELY TO SEE

COMMA
(POLYGONIA C-ALBUM)

The Comma almost made the Gardener's Favourite as its distinctive scalloped wings make it eye-catching while its adaptable life cycle allows for the vagaries of weather. It looks like a withered leaf when at rest with its wings folded, and like a raggedy Painted Lady (see page 67) when flying. The caterpillar is anything but a fussy eater and the same is true of the butterfly, which feeds happily on many garden flowers.

THE WALL
(LASIOMMATA MEGERA)

Another LBJ, easy to identify from the Gatekeeper and the Meadow Brown as it has much more elaborate black tracery across its orange wings, and several white spotted eyes. It also loves to bask, wings open, in a sunny spot such as on plants, banks or walls, hence its name.

RINGLET
(APHANTOPUS HYPERANTUS)

Similar to the Meadow Brown male (see page 72) with its darker colouring, but this is almost a velvety dark brown rather than dusky. Also, it has distinctive ringlet shapes on the underside of the wings and no pale spots on the upper side. Especially fond of damp, secluded areas.

SPECKLED WOOD
(PARARGE AEGERIA)

A beguilingly lovely, very territorial butterfly which will take up residence for several days at a time in a garden, defending its patch, courting and feeding. The speckled eyes give it perfect camouflage in dappled sunlight and it loves resting on the lower branches of trees and shrubs.

COMMON BLUE
(POLYOMMATUS ICARUS)

As its name suggests, this is the most common and widespread of several blue butterflies, albeit a low flyer which inhabits lawns and meadows, golf courses and verges. The iridescent blue males flutter about their territory looking for the females who are far less visible due to their dull brown colouring and more sedentary ways. In the evening Common Blues can become positively sociable, settling together in clusters on a host plant but favouring grassy areas.

COMMON GARDEN MOTHS

SIX SPOT BURNET
(ZYGAENA FILIPENDULAE)

Really beautiful and pleasantly slow-flying day moths, there are several Burnet moths, mainly differing in the number of their spots, five or six. It's the Six Spot that's the most common with, as the name cleverly suggests, its six red spots on each black wing. It doesn't move far or fast, and once it's set up home in your patch you tend to keep it in the garden. It especially likes long grass and scabious and knautia flowers.

GARDEN TIGER
(ARCTIA CAJA)

Named after its penchant for garden plants and its tiger-like wings of black and white, these paired with spotted under-wings of red, yellow or orange make it a spectacular sight when it flashes to deter predatory birds. It also has a handy knack of being able to secrete a noxious yellow fluid from a gland behind its head to scare off overly interested parties. Although it's a night-flying moth, you may see it in the evening, but you're also likely to spot the caterpillars, which are the classic 'woolly bear' with dark furry hair to protect them.

HUMMINGBIRD HAWK
(MACROGLOSSUM STELLATARUM)

A true wonder if you should chance to see one, as this day-flying moth literally hums as its wings beat so quickly. Common in the South of France, it migrates north during the summer in varying numbers, hovering and feeding on all sorts of garden plants such as buddleia, phlox and sweet tobacco, before darting off to another bloom.

ANGLE SHADES
(PHLOGOPHORA METICULOSA)

A common visitor to gardens which I dare say you will have seen already without knowing what to call it. With pinky-brown camouflaged, scalloped wings, it has a delicate beauty. These wings are held in carefully folded angles, hence the name, to make it look like a dead leaf as it rests. Its caterpillars are not fussy eaters either, so they too abound in the garden.

ELEPHANT HAWK
(DEILEPHILA ELPENOR)

An absolute beauty of a moth with the prettiest pink and yellow wings and white legs, although it's the caterpillar you're more likely to spot. The caterpillars feed on fuchsia, balsam and willowherb during the summer and its only means of defence is to retract its head, making it seem bigger and its eyespots more menacing – an 'elephant' head. The moths fly during the evening and love all sorts of garden flowers, from honeysuckle to petunias.

THE GARDENER'S FAVOURITE PLANTS FOR BUTTERFLIES

BUTTERFLY BUSH
(BUDDLEIA DAVIDII)

If you only have room for one butterfly plant in your garden, make it a buddleia. This easy-growing plant attracts all the superstars of the butterfly world as well as the less glamorous but equally enchanting species. It hails from China but is a real toughie in the garden, coping with almost anything and flowering reliably year after year – just what the gardener and the butterfly both require. The flowers seem to be the perfect shape for the butterfly proboscis and there are plenty of them, making it a one-stop fuelling station which means the butterflies hang around rather conveniently so you can see them. There are lots of different varieties too, some suitable for patio containers and small gardens and quite a few with 'Awards of Garden Merit' from the Royal Horticultural Society. Bear in mind that butterflies seem to prefer the lavender-blue shades rather than the darker forms.

BEST VARIETIES: 'Lochinch' has super silvery foliage and soft lavender flowers, while 'Santana' has lemon and lime variegated leaves with dark flowers. For something really spectacular, go for *Buddleia globosa* with its pom-poms of orange flowers (although it doesn't have quite the same allure for butterflies as *B. davidii*).

TIMING: Flowers repeatedly from mid summer to autumn. If you have room, grow a few varieties to extend the season. Bear in mind that it doesn't have the shapeliest growing habit so it's better with a few herbaceous plants in the foreground to hide the base, so all you see are the arching flowering stems.

LOCATION: A sunny spot towards the back of the border. Great for poor soil areas or awkward spots where little else will thrive.

PLANTING PARTNERS: Makes a lovely addition to the late summer flower or shrub border, combining well with roses, asters and many other plants.

NEED TO KNOW: Buddleia is an easy and forgiving plant to grow, but it does need a firm hand when pruning or it will out-grow its allotted space. You can also prolong the flowering period by staging your pruning over a few weeks. Deadheading also helps extend the flowering season.

BUTTERFLIES: All the showy late summer stars such as Peacock, Comma, Red Admiral and Small Tortoiseshell, as well as many others such as the Large and Small Whites.

ICE PLANT
(HYLOTELEPHIUM OR SEDUM)

The ice plant is a brilliant garden plant with its succulent blue-green foliage topped with long-lasting domed flowers in shades of pink, red or white. It grows to a very manageable height of 50cm (20in) or thereabouts and, although it's a late bloomer, often flowering very late in the summer almost into autumn, its dense, bold foliage looks good in the border before flowering too. Choose a pink variety (the best colour for butterflies anyway) and the sturdy flower heads change colour rather charmingly as they age too, starting off rose-pink and taking on russet tones as they mature.

BEST VARIETIES: Many of the cultivated forms aren't great for attracting butterflies, but the best is a selection of the plain species *Sedum spectabile* or simply the species itself.

TIMING: Flowers in late summer and well into the autumn. Leave the flower heads, as they look shapely and interesting long into the autumn.

LOCATION: Another sun worshipper, this grows best towards the front of the border and is extremely tolerant of dry soil and drought conditions.

PLANTING PARTNERS: Looks great with grasses and in rock gardens or raised beds.

NEED TO KNOW: It is a bit of a flopper on occasion, especially in a richer soil, and responds well to a hard cut back in late spring to encourage shorter, tougher growth.

BUTTERFLIES: Another favourite with late summer butterflies such as Peacock and Small Tortoiseshell, as well as many others.

SCABIOUS
(SCABIOSA AND KNAUTIA)

The name scabious actually covers a few different plants, both wildflowers and cultivated varieties, but as they're all great for butterflies it doesn't really matter if you don't differentiate between them. There are lots of colours to choose from, ranging through powder-blue to deep burgundy shades as well as pinks and white. Don't choose white though – it doesn't really attract the butterflies and there are so many super colours.

BEST VARIETIES: There are many brilliant garden varieties, including the delicious and easy growing 'Melton Pastels' and the Butterfly series, but *Knautia macedonica* is both a personal favourite and very popular with butterflies.

TIMING: Flowering from early to late summer in waves, especially if you deadhead frequently.

LOCATION: Very forgiving of poorer soils and happy in a lime or chalk soil too. Great for meadow or wild-style plantings.

PLANTING PARTNERS: Many of the taller varieties look fabulous in herbaceous borders combined with grasses and other herbaceous perennials, as well as shrubs such as roses. Smaller species naturalize well in meadow plantings, wild borders or rock gardens.

NEED TO KNOW: Watch out for powdery mildew – a white powdery spotting on the leaves, which can have a very disfiguring effect on plants in poorer soils and in dry summers. Water and mulch if you suspect the plant is vulnerable.

BUTTERFLIES: Many of the smaller moths and butterflies are attracted to scabious, especially in a wild planting with grasses.

VERBENA
(VERBENA BONARIENSIS)

This stately perennial is a firm favourite among gardeners and butterflies alike. Easy to grow and happy to seed itself around the garden, it's a winner for everyone. The flowers, though small, are nonetheless plentiful and rich in nectar and held up on surprisingly sturdy 1.5m (60in) stems, nice and tall for the butterflies to perch on.

BEST VARIETIES: This is the best species so that keeps things simple, but many of the others are also attractive to bees and butterflies.

TIMING: Flowering from summer into autumn steadily, especially if deadheaded.

LOCATION: Needs a sunny, warm spot to thrive, although it's very forgiving of poorer soils and is more than happy in a lime or chalk soil too. It's invaluable for wild-style plantings and adds unmistakable drama to any garden.

PLANTING PARTNERS: This tall and elegant species looks fabulous in herbaceous borders combined with grasses and other herbaceous perennials, as well as dotted in between paving or in gravel gardens.

NEED TO KNOW: Although it's often short-lived, it's easy to grow from seed and will seed freely around the garden or in the compost heap.

BUTTERFLIES: All the common late season butterflies, including Red Admiral, Large White, Comma, Clouded Yellow, Small White and Common Blue.

MICHAELMAS DAISY
(ASTER OR SYMPHYOTRICHUM)

There are hundreds of michaelmas daisy varieties to choose from and something to suit most gardens. They range in height from 20cm (8in) up to a whopping 1.2m (48in) and have a hugely long flowering period from mid summer through until the very end of autumn, depending on the variety. A word of warning though – many are prone to disfiguring mildew in dry seasons and soils so it's best to pick one of the slightly earlier flowering, mildew-resistant European *Aster amellus* varieties as your first to grow. These are often shorter anyway, so they are easier to fit in to a border and don't need troublesome staking. The colour range is wide, varying from white and soft pinks through to deep purple, vivid pink and night sky blue. Flower sizes vary too, from broad flat daisies 4–5cm (1½–2in) across to tiny starry flowers studded all the way up and down the stems.

BEST VARIETIES: *Aster amellus* 'King George' is a personal favourite, with large, dusty blue, single flowers with attractive yellow centres. It starts flowering in mid summer just when the butterflies are around too. For later flowering, look out for pale blue 'Little Carlow', surprisingly tall at 90cm (35in), and 'Alma Potschke', a classic with rich pink flowers.

TIMING: A long, late flowering season, especially if you grow a few varieties. *Aster amellus* starts in July and August, while the taller types such as 'Little Carlow' will go on into October.

LOCATION: Asters need a good fertile soil in which to thrive, one that doesn't dry out in late summer but is still in a nice sunny spot. Forget them if you have thin soils, unless you add plenty of leaf mould and organic matter.

PLANTING PARTNERS: Many of the taller varieties look fabulous in prairie-style borders combined with tall grasses and late-flowering rudbeckia and hydrangeas.

NEED TO KNOW: Single varieties are always best for butterflies as the yellow centres are advertising the nectar. There are two other main forms of Aster – the New Englands (*novae-angliae*) which are lovely and robust, and the New Yorks (*novae-belgii*), horribly prone to mildew and to be avoided.

BUTTERFLIES: All the late butterflies such as Small Tortoiseshell, Peacock and Red Admiral, as well as the less showy ones including the LBJs (little brown jobs).

RED VALERIAN
(CENTRANTHUS RUBER)

You'll recognize valerian from growing wild on walls and waste ground all over the place, but don't let its wild ways make you discount it as a garden plant. For one thing, it starts flowering as soon as spring gets going, the fleshy blue-green stems topped with flowers in shades of red, pink and white attracting all the early butterflies and bees. For another, it will flower again in late summer, especially if cut back in mid summer. Finally, it will flourish in the poorest, thinnest soil imaginable, often looking its best by staying shorter and more compact in a sunny, dry spot.

BEST VARIETIES: Only one species so that keeps things simple.

TIMING: Flowering from spring into autumn steadily, especially if cut back.

LOCATION: Needs a sunny, warm spot to really thrive, although it's very forgiving of situation and soil. It adds a touch of romance and wildness to the garden if used carefully.

PLANTING PARTNERS: Looks great with rocks, paving, gravel and all the plants that go well in those environments, such as grasses and other natural-looking herbaceous perennials.

NEED TO KNOW: Don't confuse it with true valerian, *Valeriana officinalis*, a good plant but with completely different growth habits and characteristics.

BUTTERFLIES: All the common garden butterflies, including Meadow Brown, Gatekeeper, Small Tortoiseshell and Painted Lady, as well as the early spring ones such as Brimstone and Orange Tip.

PERENNIAL WALLFLOWER
(ERYSIMUM)

Simply a great garden plant with a long season of flowering and very attractive to butterflies – what's not to like? This is basically a woody wallflower with a great deal of toughness and a brilliant tolerance for poor soil. Flowering from spring right through the season, if deadheaded regularly, *Erysimum* attracts all the butterflies that love the cabbage family – and that's quite a few.

BEST VARIETIES: There are lots of varieties to choose from, but you really can't beat the old reliable 'Bowles's Mauve' with its elegant flowers, dusky foliage and repeat flowering capabilities. I'm very fond of 'Red Jep' for its brilliant crimson and purple flowers, but it may not be such a winner for the butterflies.

TIMING: Flowering from late spring into autumn steadily, especially if deadheaded.

LOCATION: Needs good garden soil and a sunny, warm spot.

PLANTING PARTNERS: This is one of those plants that looks good with almost anything and in any situation. I've grown it in the border with perennials and roses, in large containers with bedding plants or on its own as a mini hedge.

NEED TO KNOW: They're often short-lived, but so easy to propagate from cuttings so it's worth having a go yourself.

BUTTERFLIES: All the common garden butterflies, including the early spring ones such as Brimstone and Orange Tip.

MARJORAM
(ORIGANUM)

While it won't set your garden alight with colour and flower power, the humble marjoram is brilliant for all sorts of pollinating insects including bees, hoverflies and butterflies. Its long flowering period, neat growth habit and unfussy good looks make it an easy-to-live-with perennial which isn't out of place in the flower border. Though small, the flowers are very rich in nectar and it's an essential herb for the kitchen garden.

BEST VARIETIES: Truth
be told, the varieties are all a bit
similar but 'Herrenhausen' and
'Rosenkuppel' have rosy-pink
flowers and an 'Award of Garden
Merit' which is always reassuring.
My favourite for the garden is the
golden-leafed 'Aureum', also with an AGM,
still great for cooking but perhaps without
quite as much pulling power for butterflies.

TIMING: Flowering from summer into early autumn.

LOCATION: Needs a sunny, warm spot.

PLANTING PARTNERS: A great plant for edging a border,
especially the golden form. Looks lovely with paving and gravel
and adds interest and colour in the kitchen garden, especially under
wall-trained fruit trees.

NEED TO KNOW: When it comes to cooking, there's sweet
marjoram, pot marjoram and oregano, all under the same Latin name.
All are edible; the flavour just varies in strength and pungency.

BUTTERFLIES: All the common garden butterflies, including
Gatekeeper, Meadow Brown, Common Blue and Small Tortoiseshell.

LAVENDER
(LAVENDULA)

Already a firm garden favourite, this plant needs little introduction to most gardeners. Evergreen, long-flowering and beautifully scented with a few varieties to choose from, there's a lavender to suit most gardens. Having said that, no lavender likes shade or damp, soggy soil, so pick a sunny, well-drained spot.

BEST VARIETIES: 'Hidcote' is the classic tall English lavender with purple-blue flowers. 'Munstead' is shorter and more compact, as is 'Imperial Gem'.

TIMING: Reliable and often extremely showy flowering when grown in a sunny spot, from mid summer into early autumn.

LOCATION: Needs a sunny, warm spot with well-drained soil to really thrive. Makes a great hedge or border to paths or lawns and looks good with all sorts of stone: rocks, paving or gravel.

PLANTING PARTNERS: Adds a definite note of country garden romance and goes brilliantly with all those sorts of plants from roses to sweet peas, irises to asters. Mediterranean dry-style plantings also work well, combined with other herbs, grasses and sun-loving shrubs and perennials.

NEED TO KNOW: Lavender tends to get open and leggy after a few years and is best replaced. Although you can cut it back, it tends to take a few years to recover.

BUTTERFLIES: All the common late-season garden butterflies, including Large White and Gatekeeper.

THISTLE
(ECHINOPS, CIRSIUM, ERYNGIUM ETC)

Not the obvious choice for a garden at first glance but, once you start looking at thistles, there are quite a few I would happily give bed and border space to for their flower power as well as their bee and butterfly allure. The globe thistle, *Echinops*, is a firm favourite for its steel-blue spherical flowers, although it needs a bit of space. For the smaller garden, the sea holly, *Eryngium*, packs the same blue punch and pulls in the butterflies and bees too. I'm a huge fan of the Scotch thistle, *Onopordum*, with its massive candelabra structure around 2m (79in) tall although it is fiercely spiky and is also biennial, flowering in the second year after sowing, and then dying.

BEST VARIETIES: Most globe thistles are pretty tall at around 1.2m (80in), but 'Veitch's Blue' is an easier-to-manage 1m (39in) in height. With attractive magenta flowers, *Cirsium* 'Atropurpureum' loves a damp spot and is positively dainty looking compared to most thistles. There are lots of sea holly varieties to choose from – all good but with different heights and characteristics, and some of them an almost luminous blue.

TIMING: Flowering in summer.

LOCATION: Thistles thrive in a sunny, warm spot with well-drained soil that's quite poor or even stony.

PLANTING PARTNERS: Spiky and dramatic, thistles add a modern touch to any planting scheme and look great with topiary shapes and bold plantings of grasses.

NEED TO KNOW: Sea holly isn't actually a true thistle – it's actually a relative of the carrot!

BUTTERFLIES: Many common butterflies, including Brimstone, Meadow Brown, Gatekeeper, Painted Lady and Large White.

CHAPTER SEVEN

MORE BRILLIANT BUTTERFLY PLANTS

G ardening is always about compromise and adjustment, especially so when space is limited. The chances are that you probably have a garden full of plants already and just want to add in some new elements to attract butterflies in quite specific areas, such as the kitchen garden or the patio. Besides this, those top must-have plants that appeal to butterflies listed in the previous chapter may not be your ideal plant choices for your garden; they might be too big, too small or just not appeal to you.

Doubtlessly, too, there will be some things you must consider above and beyond butterflies when planning your garden and so you'll need more plants to choose from than just those already mentioned. Although each garden is different from another, there are a few elements that we all want to include in our gardens, whether that's a few vegetables and herbs, some good plants for fences or butterfly-friendly plants for containers. Treat the following suggestions as something of a pick-and-mix – a selection of ideas that you can mix and match to suit your space and inclination and to make the most of your garden.

POTS, CONTAINERS AND WINDOW BOXES

You can still do a lot to attract butterflies even if you don't have a garden as such or if it's so tiny you only have room for a handful of pots and containers. In many ways this gives you a great opportunity to ring the changes, swapping nectar-rich plants season by season and placing plants deliberately close to windows and patios where you can hopefully enjoy the butterflies coming and going.

Remember the golden rules:

• Butterflies love sunshine and wind shelter, as do many plants grown in containers.

• Plant lots of different plants in your containers and cluster them closely together.

• Butterflies like a nice, dense patch of nectar-rich plants in a block so they can flutter from flower to flower.

• Go for plants of different heights – not only will it look pleasing to the eye, but it's also great for maximizing the space you have and for tempting the butterflies in over a fence or wall.

SHRUBS

While it's usually annuals that are common as container plants, don't let that prevent you from growing a few herbs or even shrubs if you have the space. Many smaller shrubs will do well in larger containers for a couple of years at least and look wonderful augmented with a few flowering annuals added to the mix.

For larger pots, think of flowering shrubs such as hebe, many of which are nicely compact but flower for a long season. Good varieties include 'Margret' with blue flowers. I'm also very fond of the more compact, patio-sized buddleias (see page 78), such as the 'Buzz' series which has been specially bred for growing in containers.

The great thing about container gardening is that you can add in some tender plants such as fragrant lantana, a great conservatory plant which does wonderfully well outdoors in the summer in a sheltered spot. This little shrub is brilliant in hot weather, resisting drought and flowering beautifully all summer.

PERENNIALS

You might be surprised how well many perennials will do in larger containers. But remember that you want a long flowering season and a good return on your investment if you only have a small space. You don't want something that will sit there leafy and dull for most of the season, throwing up the odd bloom in the height of the summer when you could have had annuals flowering madly for a month or so already.

Go for good, reliable favourites for butterflies, such as scabious and the smaller varieties of knautia, like 'Mars Midget' which will drop into pots and look great with shrubs and annuals. Or use something like anise hyssop which is a magnet for both bees and butterflies with its upright stalks of bottle-brush flowers in shades of blue and purple.

HERBS

There are the obvious herb choices, particularly rosemary and lavender (see page 90) which do well in containers, but most of the herbs are good in pots and boxes. Marjoram (see page 88), chives and so on all seem to thrive in containers, and it's one of the best ways to grow mint as it can be far too invasive if grown in a border or bed. Clusters of potted herbs look great alone, or even better when combined with annuals for a seasonal splash of colour.

HANDY HERB WINDOW BOX
This grouping of herbs will work well in a window box, providing interest for both you and the butterflies with different leaf shapes and colours:
Small rosemary
Broad-leafed thyme
Chives
Violas

ANNUALS

As for the annuals, many are a bit lacking in nectar but there are a few very good choices. Top of my list is cosmos, a brilliant garden plant which is also great in containers, long flowering and extremely showy as long as you deadhead regularly. I love their sugared-almond pink-and-white flowers and their feathery foliage. Stick to the single or semi-double varieties, where the nectar-rich yellow stamens are easy for the butterfly to spot.

For early in the season, violas, primroses and wallflowers (see page 87) are all good nectar choices and will cheer the early spring garden. Following on from these, forget-me-nots and the tiny blooms of alyssum are an absolute must-have for the container garden. Although alyssum is miniature, the flowers are so wonderfully scented that they fill the garden with the aroma of honey, attracting bees and butterflies in profusion.

Don't forget the good old nasturtium either, which is great for containers and so easy to grow. There are several lovely compact varieties which are perfect for containers, such as 'Cherry Rose' and 'Black Velvet'.

FOUR-SEASON WINDOW BOX

Window boxes can provide a pretty outlook all year round, but it can be expensive to plant them from scratch as each new season arrives. My 'recipe' below uses hebe as the main plant to provide structure, along with golden marjoram for year-round interest, with other butterfly-friendly filler plants added in each season.

SPRING RECIPE
Hebe, as main structure plant
Golden marjoram
Blue violas
Cream primroses
Blue forget-me-nots
Tête-à-Tête daffodils

SUMMER REFRESH
Hebe, as main structure plant
Golden marjoram
Blue lobelia
Pink dianthus or scabious
Alyssum

AUTUMN/WINTER INTEREST
Hebe, as main structure plant
Golden marjoram
Ornamental grass
White and purple violas
'Sugar Rush purple' wallflower

CHECKLIST
- **Shrubs:** buddleia 'Buzz', hebe 'Margret', lantana
- **Perennials:** anise hyssop, dianthus, knautia, scabious
- **Herbs:** chive, lavender, marjoram, mint, rosemary
- **Annuals:** alyssum, cosmos, forget-me-not, nasturtium, primrose, viola, wallflower

WALLS AND FENCES

Walls and fences can provide brilliant habitats for birds, bees and butterflies too. They're also useful for allowing you to extend your garden, literally climbing upwards in a bid to attract creatures into your domain. Think of your fences and walls as additional planting spaces – leaving them bare does nothing for you or the wildlife.

• Use trellises to provide additional height, allowing you to train shrubs such as Japanese quince and firethorn in a confined space. Not only do these shrubs flower beautifully, but they also provide fruit for wildlife later in the season.

• Make the most of large planters for more shrubs and even small trees. Many trees are good for butterflies, particularly holly and fruit trees.

• Plant wall-trained fruit such as an espalier-trained apple or a fan-trained currant bush. There will be flowers and fruit for both you and the butterflies to enjoy, especially if you leave some windfalls to rot, which many of the late season butterflies love.

• Add in feeding and water stations at intervals on the fence, where you can place a shallow saucer of water for butterflies to drink, and the odd over-ripe plum or apple for them to enjoy.

LIVING WALLS

Brilliant for smaller gardens, living walls are becoming increasingly popular to make the most from limited space. They're widely used in urban commercial sites as a way to 'green the cityscape' and can be planted with a wide range of plants. The plants are grown in a structure that is fixed to the wall and allows non-climbing plants to grow on a vertical surface.

Choosing the plants is slightly tricky as it depends on aspect and the microclimate of the wall but there are lots of options, from perennials, grasses, herbs and even fruit and vegetables. Try including scented plants, flowering annuals and, of course, herbs such as marjoram, but talk to your local garden nursery about plants that will suit the aspect and microclimate of the wall on which they will be grown.

SHELVES AND LADDERS

An easy way to break up a dull fence or wall with planting is simply to put up some shelves. Make sure they're wide and sturdy enough to support pots and containers, which can be planted with annuals, perennials and herbs.

In the same way, an old wooden stepladder, can be used to support plank shelves with pots and boxes of plants.

THE BEST CLIMBERS

Bramble easily tops this list and nearly made it into The Gardener's Favourite Plants for Butterflies (see pages 78–93), only missing out because it's not the sort of thing most of us want in our garden. Having said that, it is a magnificent butterfly plant, often inundated with Gatekeepers when in flower and very popular in autumn for its succulent fruit too. There are some attractive and, more importantly, thornless commercial varieties which look great in the kitchen garden but also make quite a feature when well trained and managed on a fence. Varieties like 'Loch Ness' have large, crinkled flowers in a delicate shade of pink-tinged white, followed by the best and biggest blackberries you will ever eat.

Ivy, especially varieties derived from native species, makes a great climber for an ugly wall or fence, and the flowering varieties are wonderful for feeding butterflies and moths later in the year. Even the leafy forms of ivy provide excellent shelter for chrysalises and for butterflies such as Brimstone to hide themselves among the leaves for a rest. All forms of ivy are home to the eggs and caterpillars of the Holly Blue butterfly.

Hops, too, are brilliant caterpillar food plants although rather a rampageous grower. I'd be inclined to opt for the golden hop, *Humulus lupulus* 'Aureus', which has rather a good lime-green colour and seems to be just as munchable to caterpillars. It's a host plant to many species of moth and butterfly larvae, including the rather lovely Comma butterfly.

For a real seasonal splash of colour, plant a nasturtium 'Jewel of Africa'. This is the climbing, trailing exuberant form with brilliantly coloured flowers and white splashed leaves. It practically grows as you watch it and White butterflies love it.

Don't forget the humble honeysuckle too. It's not especially good for attracting butterflies, but very good for moths, with its strong evening scent.

CHECKLIST
- **Trees and shrubs:** firethorn, holly, Japanese quince, trained fruit trees and currants
- **Herbs:** marjoram, mint, thyme
- **Annuals:** calendula, lobelia, nasturtium, viola
- **Climbers:** honeysuckle, hops, ivy, nasturtium 'Jewel of Africa', ornamental bramble

SMALL SPACES

Just because a garden is small, it doesn't mean that you can't provide pretty much all the habitats that butterflies adore. Okay, you can't provide that sweeping hay meadow or wild expanse of flowering grasses and wild flowers that many butterflies use as food plants for their caterpillars, but you can make a mini meadow, allowing a patch of lawn to grow out and inter-planting it with wild flowers. Perhaps you could introduce shade-loving wild flowers in that dark corner under the hedge, or plant a few flowering herbs in the odd sunny spot by the shed. You could even get a few plants such as a creeping thyme and dwarf dianthus growing in between the paving slabs of the patio – not only are these little flowering plants brilliant for butterflies, but they'll also soften the harsh edges of the stone and break up the broad expanse.

A small garden can also be transformed quickly and without it costing a fortune. It just needs some thought about the elements you already have, some planning to introduce a few other essentials and some good old-fashioned effort to bring it all together.

LAYERED PLANTING

In a small garden you can really make the most of layered planting. The top layer could be a small tree or a couple of climbers trained over arches or an arbour; the next layer is a handful of small shrubs, a hedge and taller herbaceous perennials, and at the bottom is the ground-level planting of smaller plants and grass. Choose the plants carefully, paying close attention to their eventual size, and you can create a perfect little oasis for butterflies in your small garden.

CHOOSE DWARF AND MINI VARIETIES OF PLANTS

These days with so many of us having small gardens, nurseries are developing lots of smaller varieties of well-loved plants. For example, the Buzz series of compact buddleias is a great introduction as most buddleias are on the large side. Look out for any varieties of plant that are described as dwarf, compact or patio-sized, although bear in mind you don't want everything too small or it will look like a model village!

PLANT A TREE

Even in a small garden the height and structure a tree gives your garden is invaluable. Also, it's a great place for birds to perch and butterflies to rest. If it's a flowering tree such as a fruit tree, even better. Fruit trees are available on different sized rootstocks and these are brilliant for spring blossom nectar. Later on, the rotting fruit is especially attractive to Peacocks and Red Admirals.

MAKE A MINI MEADOW

In a small garden this is more a case of letting your lawn go wild as there probably isn't room for both lawn and meadow. A well-kept lawn really is a monoculture, a barren wasteland of grass which isn't allowed to flower. By comparison, a meadow is a rich tapestry of flowering plants and grasses which provides a home to all sorts of creatures. A meadow is definitely the best for butterflies. So stop treating your lawn, allow the clover to come back in and hopefully a few other plants too, and let it grow.

GET CREATIVE

The great thing about a small garden is that it doesn't take much time, effort or money to transform it. The joy is in the detail: that little butterfly house nestled in the climber on the back fence, the glazed saucer of water on the stone among the echinacea for the butterflies to drink from, and the window box of flowering herbs under the sunny kitchen window. All this would vanish in the sheer scale of a larger garden, so savour the smallness.

COLOUR-THEMED POTS

If you like to plant your pots and containers by colour, try these butterfly-winning combinations. The pink 'recipe' works well for a pot or a small border.

A LITTLE POT OF SUNSHINE
Spirea 'Goldflame'
Calendula
Quaking grass
Golden marjoram
Bidens

IN THE PINK
Dwarf apple tree 'Red Falstaff' or 'Saturn'
Scabious 'Pink Butterfly'
Marjoram 'Herrenhausen'
Sweet William

CHECKLIST
- **Trees and shrubs:** buddleia 'Buzz', dwarf and trained fruit trees, spiraea, compact varieties
- **Perennials:** dianthus, echinacea, gaura, grasses, wild flowers
- **Herbs:** chive, marjoram, thyme
- **Annuals:** lobelia, marigold, viola

LARGER GARDENS

A large garden obviously gives you all the potential you could ever wish for to create a complete butterfly haven. Not only have you got plenty of room for lovely big borders filled with a long season of herbaceous perennials flowering for all they're worth, but you also have space for the bigger growing shrubs such as buddleia and flowering currant. You can plant a veritable orchard of fruit trees which is perfect for attracting early butterflies when in flower, and also just as attractive at the other end of the season for their fruit.

A large garden really is a great thing to have. But, as with all things, there is one drawback and that is the sheer scale. In a large garden you can lose that proximity to butterflies which is inevitable in a smaller space. The butterflies may well be there but flitting about in the further reaches of the garden rather than close by where you might get a chance to see them. But there are a few little tricks which should help bring them closer to you.

REPEAT PLANTS

Plant a few buddleias, dotting them in the borders throughout the garden, with some closer to paths and the patio. This will encourage the butterflies to flit and feed and should give you a good chance to observe them. There are all sorts of plants that can be used this way, from the smaller ice plant to bulbs such as alliums and even up to trees and shrubs like buddleia and holly. They don't need to all be the same variety, or even the same species.

Repeat trees by planting a little copse of natives such as hawthorn and rowan. My favourite is an orchard of fruit trees with long grass and wild flowers beneath. Not only is it good for the wildlife, but repeating plants in a large garden also makes the space look more cohesive and planned rather than cluttered.

If you are planning a border from scratch, or filling in gaps in an existing border, try these planting combinations.

PURPLE AND WHITE BORDER
Buddleia davidii 'Lochinch'
White willowherb
Aster 'Violet Queen'
Sweet rocket or honesty
Allium 'Purple Sensation'

WILDFLOWER WINNERS FOR THE BORDER
These will drop into flower borders without looking too 'wild'.
Yarrow
Cornflower
Red campion
Quaking grass
Cowslips and primroses or primula
Violas

MAKE A MEADOW

An absolute essential if you have plenty of room. Not only are there all those wild flowers that butterflies love, but many of the 'wilder' butterflies feed on the flowers of different grasses which are exactly what makes a true meadow.

Create a meadow fairly close to the house with mown paths through it so you can wander through and spot the butterflies feeding and flirting. Plant a really good succession of wild flowers – nothing fancy, just good old bird's-foot trefoil, knapweed, scabious and other butterfly favourites.

A large garden gives you a great opportunity to create different meadow habitats. Making a hay meadow is a must for an area in the full sun, but the dappled shade areas at the edges of your copse or hedgerow are also ideal for creating habitats for butterflies such as the Speckled Wood. Plant here with different, more shade-loving wild flowers such as campion, garlic mustard and primrose.

PLANT HEDGES

Every garden needs a boundary, and while smaller gardens can't afford the space a hedge takes up, they're the perfect surround for a larger garden. Some 39 species of butterfly are recorded in UK hedgerows and 20 of those use hedgerows as their breeding grounds, so it's well worth having a good hedge.

There are lots of plants to choose from, such as native hedges like beech and hawthorn which are fantastic for wildlife and also create sheltered, warm spaces which the butterflies love. Go for a mixed country-style hedge of blackthorn, hawthorn, dogwood and field rose and, not only will you have a garden of fantastic flowers and nectar for the adult butterflies, you will also be providing brilliant food plants for caterpillars. It might not be the neatest or most orderly hedge, but it will be the absolute best for wildlife. Or you can stick to one species such as holly or hawthorn for a more refined look.

Even better, use hedges to divide a large garden into smaller, more intimate spaces. Creating garden 'rooms' is a classic garden design trick to section up a large space and each 'room' can have its own theme or concept, such as the kitchen garden, the herb garden, the cut flower garden and so on. Each hedge around the room gives the butterflies plenty of hiding places from predators as well as creating a sheltered, enclosed environment protected from the wind, bathed in sunshine and full of nectar-rich plants.

CREATE A POND AND STREAM

There is nothing that attracts wildlife as much as water. Butterflies love water, especially shallow, muddy edges to watercourses where they can drink. A pond will also encourage birds, frogs, toads and dragonflies to visit your garden.

It doesn't need to be big but it does need to be in a sunny spot away from trees. It should also link up with other wildlife features in the garden such as log piles, long grass and hedges. You can also use marginal planting around the edges such as yellow flag iris, water forget-me-not and marsh marigold to help achieve this. Those edges should be shallow and shelved to allow wildlife easy access, with a few rocks or logs for perching. Ideally most of the pond should only be 30cm (12in) or so deep, with a deeper area of about 60cm (24in). A boggy area and a little water movement are good too – try a shallow stream or waterfall, a small sprinkly fountain or just a little bubble-up through some rocks.

THINK BIG

You have the room, so go for those really big, bold blocks of plants and opt for large varieties too. Remember that butterflies like a nice palette of interesting nectars to choose from, so plant some really deep borders. With all that space you can afford to plant the imposing hemp agrimony with some abandon and have stands of tall globe thistles along with an array of tall asters. This is the only chance you'll have to grow the beautiful white willowherb because it's a tad invasive (like its pink cousin), but in a large garden you can happily devote a corner to it without worrying that it will take over the whole garden.

NETTLES

None of us really want nettles in our garden by choice, but they're unbeatable as a caterpillar food plant. Small Tortoiseshell, Red Admiral, Peacock and all sorts of other butterflies home in on nettle patches for laying their eggs. At least in a large garden there's room to leave an unkempt patch behind the garage or next to the compost heap, or even cultivate a few nettles lurking by the shed. Turn a blind eye and just think of the butterflies.

CHECKLIST

- **Trees and shrubs:** flowering currant, hawthorn, rowan, fruit trees, field rose, dogwood, beech
- **Perennials:** ice plant, scabious, hemp agrimony, globe thistle, asters, white willowherb, primroses
- **Herbs:** fennel, sorrel, garlic mustard, mint
- **Wildflowers:** red campion, knapweed, bird's-foot trefoil, grasses
- **Pond plants:** yellow flag iris, water mint, water forget-me-not, marsh marigold
- **Annuals:** cosmos, single-flowered dahlias, honesty, sweet rocket

ALLOTMENTS AND KITCHEN GARDENS

Butterflies are brilliant pollinators, not perhaps in quite the same league as bees but no slow coaches, so encouraging them into the productive garden helps considerably with flower and fruit set. Fortunately, butterflies are also very mobile and love all sorts of flowers which are easily incorporated into beds without reducing productive space and adding hugely to the beauty of the kitchen garden or allotment.

Encouraging butterflies into your allotment or kitchen garden may seem at first something you really don't want to do – I picture white butterflies fluttering around my young cabbage and kale plants, spelling doom for their later survival. But it's important to understand what motivates butterflies and moths, good and bad, so you can actively encourage or discourage accordingly.

CABBAGE BUTTERFLIES
Small Whites lay their eggs singly, which means they're less easy to spot than the Large White eggs in their clusters. The same is true of the caterpillars as the Large Whites decimate en masse, while the Small Whites hide in the middle of your cabbage plants looking like fresh green growth. The reason the adults favour brassicas for their eggs is due to the mustard oils contained in the plant. The ravenous caterpillars then accumulate the mustard oil in their bodies, which makes them extremely distasteful and smell very unpleasant – all in all, not an attractive nibble to a bird.

I've spent many a time scrutinizing plants, removing the caterpillars and, once I realized the birds don't eat them due to their bad taste, squashing them ruthlessly. It's an awful task which I no longer need to do thanks to a nearby planting of nasturtiums and garlic mustard. They seem to enjoy these as a food plant almost as much as my precious cabbages and, as the nasturtiums run amok across the kitchen garden, I'm quite happy for the White butterfly caterpillars to eat their fill. In an ideal world, the butterflies would lay their eggs directly on these decoy plants. Of course, typically, nature is not perfect, but at least I have somewhere to deposit the pests and the cabbages stand a better chance than before. Besides that, the nasturtiums are also useful for keeping blackfly off the later fruiting broad beans and both the flowers and leaves are good for us to eat as well.

ANNUAL FLOWERS
Easy-to-grow annuals such as calendula, borage, cornflower and viola are great for filling in gaps between vegetables and some make lovely cut flowers, too. Growing an entire bed of the same thing makes it extremely easy for pests to find a crop so by adding in a few flowers you can confuse the pests while attracting butterflies at the same time.

POLLINATOR WINNERS TO DROP INTO
VEGETABLE BEDS
*Add a few of these between the rows to pull in pollinators
and predatory insects.*
Anise hyssop
Borage
Chives
Cornflowers
Cosmos
Poached egg plant
Rocket
Violas

MORE PESTS

Of course, quite a number of those pests are moths. As well as the Large and Small White butterflies interfering with your brassicas, there are quite a number of moths which are all too familiar to anyone who grows fruit and vegetables for more than a few seasons – Leek, Pea, Plum, Tortrix and Codling moth are just a few of the most common. However, there are ways of outwitting them. For example, growing an early crop of peas means that you're harvesting before the adult moth is laying eggs. Planting leeks with carrots works twofold as the carrot smell confuses the leek moth and the leek smell puts off the carrot fly. Codling moths aren't usually too much of a problem, but you can trap the male moths with pheromone traps. This lures the male into the trap by using the 'scent' or pheromone of the female and so reduces successful mating. But don't forget that as well as this handful of nuisances, there are thousands of completely harmless and some very beneficial moths out there.

PLANT LOTS OF HERBS

One of the easiest ways to pull in pollinators of all sorts into the kitchen garden is by planting lots of herbs. Herbs are brilliant plants with often a long flowering season and very nectar-rich flowers. Chives, mint, marjoram and thyme are some of the most common culinary herbs that are easy to grow and great to have on hand for creative cooking, but the list is almost endless. Finding a space for some of the more elegant shrubs such as lemon verbena, rosemary and, of course, lavender, is surprisingly easy as they combine so well with other plants and add structure and an air of permanence to the kitchen garden.

CROPS IN POTS

If your outdoor space doesn't have room for a dedicated kitchen garden, there are still some butterfly-friendly crops which grow well in containers – even dwarf fruit trees. The following list of plants is a good starting point.

EASY EDIBLES FOR CONTAINERS
Chives
Cut-and-come-again lettuce
Dwarf pear tree 'Concorde'
Dwarf tomato 'Totem' or 'Tumbler'
Nasturtium
Rocket
Violas

CHECKLIST

- **Trees and shrubs:** fruit trees and bushes, bramble
- **Herbs:** chive, lavender, lemon verbena, marjoram, mint, rosemary, thyme
- **Edibles:** garlic mustard, rocket
- **Flowers:** borage, calendula, cornflower, nasturtium, viola

CHAPTER EIGHT

RESOURCES

Hopefully everything you've read so far has whetted your appetite for all things butterfly, but there's only so much information I can squeeze into one book. Fortunately, there is a great deal of information out there on websites and blogs and in books. What follows is a purely personal selection of links and information to take you further into the world of butterfly gardening.

FOR THE UK AND EUROPE

The best place to start is with the UK organization Butterfly Conservation, a fount of information on butterflies, moths, their habitats, sightings and much other information: **butterfly-conservation.org**

There are a great many more butterflies, moths and their caterpillars to identify than I've been able to cover in this book. For brilliant identification in both UK and Europe, take a look at the following organizations and their websites:
UK Butterflies: **ukbutterflies.co.uk**
Moths and Butterflies of Europe and North Africa: **leps.it**
Butterfly Conservation Europe: **bc-europe.eu**

FOR THE USA

Butterflies of America (provides a complete guide to American butterfly species): **butterfliesofamerica.com**
North American Butterfly Association: **naba.org**
Association for Butterflies (they have awareness days and offer mini grants for butterfly projects in the US): **afbeducation.org/butterfly-conservation**
The Xerces Society (involved in invertebrate and butterfly conservation throughout the US): **xerces.org**

Learn About Butterflies (offers a comprehensive guide to butterflies throughout the world): **learnaboutbutterflies.com**

FOR CHILDREN AND TEACHING RESOURCES
Enchanted Learning (US site, but teaching resources are relevant worldwide):
enchantedlearning.com/subjects/butterfly
The Children's Butterfly Site (has activities and teaching resources): **kidsbutterfly.org**
Woodland Trust (for information on recording nature events): **naturescalendar.woodlandtrust.org.uk**

FOR BREEDING AND RECORDING EQUIPMENT
Watkins & Doncaster: **watdon.co.uk**
ALS: **angleps.com**

FOR BUTTERFLY RECORDING, HABITATS, NATURE RESERVES AND OTHER PLACES TO SEE BUTTERFLIES AND MOTHS
The Wildlife Trusts (UK county wildlife trusts): **wildlifetrusts.org**
National Trust (responsible for various coastal reserves and commons throughout England, Wales and Northern Ireland): **nationaltrust.org.uk**
National Trust for Scotland: **nts.org.uk**
The Royal Society for the Protection of Birds (bird reserves are also good for butterflies and moths): **rspb.org.uk**
Natural England:
gov.uk/government/organisations/natural-england
UK Butterfly Monitoring Scheme: **ukbms.org**

FOR MORE GARDENING, BUTTERFLY PLANTS
AND WILDFLOWER ADVICE
Royal Horticultural Society: **rhs.org.uk**
Plantlife (UK conservation charity working nationally
and internationally to save threatened wild flowers,
plants and fungi): **plantlife.org.uk/uk**
Garden Organic (advice and help to garden organically):
gardenorganic.org.uk
Wildlife Gardening Forum (aims to inspire and encourage
everyone to garden with wildlife in mind): **wlgf.org**
Gardens With Wings (US site with plant and gardening advice):
gardenswithwings.com

TO GET INVOLVED WITH GARDENING EVEN IF
YOU DON'T HAVE A GARDEN
Social Farms and Gardens (UK-wide charity supporting
communities to farm, garden and grow together):
farmgarden.org.uk
To find an allotment near you: **gov.uk/apply-allotment**

THESE ARE A FEW OF THE BOOKS I USED FOR
RESEARCH
Brickell, Christopher, *RHS A–Z Encyclopedia of Garden Plants*
(Dorling Kindersley, 2016 4th editon)

Feltwell, John, *Reader's Digest Field Guide to the Butterflies and
Other Insects of Britain* (Reader's Digest, 1983)

Moucha, Josef, *A Colour Guide to Familiar Butterflies, Caterpillars
and Chrysalides* (Littlehampton Book Services, 1974)

Tampion, John and Maureen, *Attracting Butterflies to Your Garden*
(GMC Publications, 2011)

AND FINALLY

TAKE PART IN THE BIG BUTTERFLY COUNT

Anyone can get involved in the Big Butterfly Count, and you certainly don't need to be an expert! The website has a butterfly identification chart for you to print and take out with you, or there is a free app if you prefer. So get involved – take a few minutes out of your day this summer and help to track these precious insects and protect them for generations to come. Visit **bigbutterflycount.org** and find out more about this year's count.

If you're in North America, you will find a butterfly count near you on the NABA website. There are annual volunteer butterfly counts in the weeks leading up to or after July 4 in the US, July 1 in Canada, and September 16 in Mexico. Visit **naba.org** for more information.

COMMON AND LATIN BUTTERFLY AND MOTH NAMES

A, B

Adonis Blue butterfly *Lysandra bellargus*
Angle Shades moth *Phlogophora meticulosa*
Brimstone butterfly *Gonepteryx rhamni*
Bullseye moth *Automeris io*

C, E

Cabbage White *see* Large White and Small White
Chalkhill Blue butterfly *Lysandra coridon*
Clouded Yellow butterfly *Colias croceus*
Codling moth *Cydia pomonella*
Comma butterfly *Polygonia c-album*
Common Blue butterfly *Polyommatus icarus*
Elephant Hawk moth *Deilephila elpenor*

G

Garden Tiger moth *Arctia caja*
Gatekeeper butterfly *Pyronia tithonus*
Glass-winged butterfly *Greta oto*
Green Veined White butterfly *Artogeia napi*

H

Holly Blue butterfly *Celastrina argiolus*
Hummingbird Hawk moth *Macroglossum stellatarum*

L

Large White butterfly *Pieris brassicae*
Leek moth *Acrolepiopsis assectella*

M, O

Meadow Brown butterfly *Maniola jurtina*
Monarch butterfly *Danaus plexippus*
Orange Tip butterfly *Anthocharis cardamines*

P

Painted Lady butterfly *Vanessa cardui*
Peacock butterfly *Inachis io*
Pea moth *Cydia nigricana*
Plain Tiger moth *Danaus chrysippus*
Plum moth *Grapholita (Cydia) funebrana*
Purple Emperor butterfly *Apatura iris*

Q, R

Queen Alexandra's Birdwing butterfly *Ornithoptera alexandrae*
Red Admiral butterfly *Vanessa atalanta*
Ringlet butterfly *Aphantopus hyperantus*

S

Six Spot Burnet moth *Zygaena filipendulae*
Small Copper *Lycaena phlaeas*
Small Tortoiseshell butterfly *Aglais urticae*
Small White butterfly *Pieris rapae*
Speckled Wood butterfly *Pararge aegeria*

T

The Wall butterfly *Lasiommata megera*
Tortrix moth *Cacoecimorpha pronubana* and *Epiphyas postvittana*

COMMON AND LATIN PLANT NAMES

Common names for plants can vary widely, depending on region and country. In many cases, the most widely used name for a plant is also its Latin name.

spp. *Various species*

A
Alder Buckthorn, *Frangula alnus*
Allium, *Allium* spp.
Anise Hyssop, *Agastache* spp.
Aster, *see* Michaelmas Daisy

B
Balsam, *Impatiens*
Beech, *Fagus sylvatica*
Bidens, *Bidens*
Bird's-foot Trefoil, *Lotus corniculatus*
Borage, *Borago officinalis*
Bramble, *Rubus fruticosus*
Buckthorn, *Rhamnus cathartica*
Butterfly Bush, *Buddleia davidii*

C
Calendula, *see* Pot Marigold
Campion, *see* Red Campion
Chives, *Allium schoenoprasum*
Clover, *Trifolium*

Coneflower, *Echinacea purpurea*
Cornflower, *Centaurea cyanus*
Cosmos, *Cosmos bipinnatus*
Cowslip, *Primula veris*
Crambe, *see* Sea Kale
Cuckoo Flower, *Cardamine pratensis*

D, E

Daffodil, *Narcissus*
Dahlia, *Dahlia*
Dianthus, *see* Pink
Dogwood, *Cornus sanguinea*
Echinacea, *see* Coneflower

F

Fennel, *Foeniculum vulgare*
Field Rose, *Rosa arvensis*
Firethorn, *Pyracantha coccinea*
Flowering Currant, *Ribes sanguineum*
Forget-me-not, *Myosotis arvensis*
Fruit trees, *Malus, Prunus,* etc
Fuchsia, *Fuchsia*

G

Garlic Mustard, *Alliaria petiolata*
Gaura, *Gaura lindheimeri*
Globe Thistle, *Echinops* spp.
Goldenrod, *Solidago* spp.

H

Hawthorn, *Crataegus monogyna*
Hebe, *Hebe* spp.
Hedge Mustard, *see* Garlic Mustard
Hemp Agrimony, *Eupatorium*
Holly, *Ilex* spp.
Honesty, *Lunaria annua*
Honeysuckle, *Lonicera*
Hops, *Humulus lupulus*

I, J

Ice Plant, *Hylotelephium* or *Sedum*
Ivy, *Hedera helix*
Japanese Quince, *Chaenomeles*

K

Knautia, *see* Scabious
Knapweed, *Centaurea nigra*

L

Lantana, *Lantana*
Lavender, *Lavandula angustifolia*
Lemon Verbena, *Aloysia citrodora*
Lilac, *Syringa vulgaris*
Lobelia, *Lobelia erinus*

M, N

Marigold, see Pot Marigold
Marjoram, *Origanum* varieties
Marsh Marigold, *Caltha palustris*
Michaelmas Daisy, *Aster* or *Symphyotrichum*

Mint, *Mentha* spp.
Nasturtium, *Tropaeolum*

P

Perennial Wallflower, *see* Wallflower
Petunia, *Petunia*
Phlox, *Phlox paniculata*
Pink, *Dianthus* spp.
Plantain, *Plantago*
Poached egg plant, *Limnanthes douglasii*
Pot Marigold, *Calendula officinalis*
Primrose, *Primula vulgaris*

Q

Quaking grass, *Briza maxima*

R

Red Campion, *Silene dioica*
Red Valerian, *Centranthus ruber*
Rosemary, *Rosmarinus officinalis*
Rowan, *Sorbus aucuparia*

S

Scabious, *Scabiosa* and *Knautia*
Scotch Thistle, *Onopordum*
Sea Holly, *Eryngium*
Sea Kale, *Crambe cordifolia*
Snowberry, *Symphoricarpos albus*
Sorrel, *Rumex acetosa*
Spindle, *Euonymus europaeus*
Spiraea, *Spiraea*
Stinging Nettle, *Urtica dioica*

Sweet Alyssum, *see* Alyssum
Sweet Rocket, *Hesperis matronalis*
Sweet Tobacco, *Nicotiana* spp.
Sweet William, *Dianthus barbatus*

T

Thistle, *Echinops, Cirsium, Eryngium* and many other spp.
  see also Globe Thistle, Scotch Thistle, Sea Holly
Thyme, *Thymus* spp.
Tree Mallow, *Lavatera*

V

Verbena, *Verbena bonariensis*
Violet, *Viola*

W

Wallflower, *Erysimum* spp.
Water Forget-me-not, *Myosotis scorpioides*
Water Mint, *Mentha aquatica*
Watercress, *Nasturtium officinale*
White Willowherb, *Epilobium angustifolium 'Album'*

Y

Yarrow, *Achillea millefolium*
Yellow Flag Iris, *Iris pseudacorus*

ACKNOWLEDGEMENTS

My thanks go to Jane Graham Maw and Harriet Butt and her team for all their help and to James Weston Lewis for making my words come to life with his illustrations.

A huge thank you to Richard Hood, for being a friend, and to my parents, Theo and Keith, who love gardening and encouraged me to love it too.

The biggest thanks of all must go to Anna, my right hand, and my partner Paul, who has put up with me ruining many a good walk by stopping every few minutes to gaze at fluttering things in hedgerows.

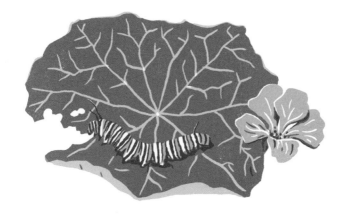

ACKNOWLEDGEMENTS

ABOUT THE AUTHOR

In a horticultural career spanning 30 years, Jane Moore has been head gardener at a Benedictine Abbey, a writer for national gardening magazines and newspapers, a researcher on BBC gardening programmes and a presenter on BBC TV's Gardeners' World. Gardening, and writing about gardening, have encompassed Jane's whole career. She has wide-ranging practical experience, an astonishingly broad plant knowledge and an unswerving enthusiasm for gardens, horticulture and its impact on everyday life.

Publishing Director Sarah Lavelle
Commissioning Editor Harriet Butt
Series Designer Maeve Bargman
Senior Designer Katherine Keeble
Illustrator James Weston Lewis
Head of Production Stephen Lang
Production Controller Sinead Hering

Published in 2020 by Quadrille,
an imprint of Hardie Grant Publishing

Quadrille
52–54 Southwark Street
London SE1 1UN
quadrille.com

Cataloguing in Publication Data: a catalogue record for
this book is available from the British Library.

Text © Jane Moore 2020
Illustrations © James Weston Lewis 2020
Design © Quadrille 2020

ISBN 978 178713 535 2

Reprinted in 2021
10 9 8 7 6 5 4 3 2
Printed in India